Seeds of a Nation

WISCONSIN

1848

Wisconsin

Michael V. Uschan

KIDHAVEN
PRESS™

THOMSON
★
GALE

San Diego • Detroit • New York • San Francisco • Cleveland
New Haven, Conn. • Waterville, Maine • London • Munich

To the students of Pleasant View Elementary School: Read to Learn!

For more information, contact
KidHaven Press
27500 Drake Rd.
Farmington Hills, MI 48331-3535
Or you can visit our Internet site at http://www.gale.com

LIBRARY OF CONGRESS CATALOGING-IN-PUBLICATION DATA

Uschan, Michael V., 1948-
  Wisconsin / by Michael V. Uschan.
    v. cm.—(Seeds of a nation)
  Includes bibliographical references and index.
  Contents: Wisconsin's first inhabitants—Explorers and fur traders—American settlers arrive—Wisconsin becomes the thirtieth state.
  ISBN 0-7377-1481-6 (lib. bdg. : alk. paper)
  1. Wisconsin—History—To 1848—Juvenile literature. [1. Wisconsin—History—To 1848.] I. Title. II. Series.
    F584 .U8   2003
    977.5—dc21
2002014469

Printed in China

Contents

A Land Carved by Ice

Wisconsin is located in the northern Midwest region of the United States. One million years ago, much of this region was covered with ice. Wisconsin's beautiful landscape was shaped during this ancient **Ice Age**. At the time, **glaciers** hundreds of feet tall covered most of the state and other parts of the Midwest.

The glaciers swept over Wisconsin four different times as the weather kept warming up and cooling down. The giant masses of ice carved the state's hills and valleys. The glaciers also dug channels and deep holes for the state's many rivers and lakes. About ten thousand years ago the glaciers began to melt. There was enough water from the melting ice to fill the rivers and more than fourteen thousand lakes that lie within Wisconsin's borders.

Wisconsin is bounded on the north by Lake Superior and the Upper Peninsula of Michigan. To the east lies Lake Michigan. To the south is the state of Illinois. To the west lie Minnesota and Iowa.

Wisconsin covers an area of 64,499 square miles. It measures 295 miles at its widest point and 320 miles at its longest. The state's weather matches its northern location. Wisconsin has long, cold winters with lots of snow, and warm but fairly short summers.

Wisconsin's **climate** suits its wildlife. The state's wild animals include white-tailed deer, wolves, black bears, rabbits, squirrels, and badgers. Wisconsin is home to many birds and a wide variety of ducks and geese as well. The bald eagle, America's national symbol, can be found in western Wisconsin along the Mississippi River. Wisconsin's lakes and rivers contain more than 170 species of fish including the **muskellunge**, a large, fierce fish that weighs up to eighty pounds.

Thousands of years ago, the richness of its land and abundant wildlife made Wisconsin an inviting home to its first human inhabitants, the **Native Americans**. Since then, many people have come to call Wisconsin home, and everyone shares in its treasures.

The powerful muskellunge is commonly found in Wisconsin's many lakes and rivers.

Chapter One

Wisconsin's First Inhabitants

The first people to live in Wisconsin arrived more than twelve thousand years ago. They were descendants of men and women who had **migrated** to the northwestern part of North America from Asia more than twenty thousand years ago.

Over thousands of years, these early inhabitants, or Native Americans, and their descendants moved south and east across America in search of food and new places to live. Some of these Native American groups, or Indian tribes, settled in the Midwest, including Wisconsin.

First Inhabitants

When Native Americans reached Wisconsin, they discovered a rich land with thousands of small lakes and rivers. The many animals and fish that live in or near the rivers became the Indians' main source of food. However, the people also ate nuts and berries that grew naturally in the wild.

Wisconsin's first residents lived in small groups of fifteen to forty in caves or temporary huts made of animal skin. The climate was still very cold, and Ice Age glaciers still covered northern Wisconsin. The people moved often to find animals to hunt. Some of the creatures they hunted are now **extinct**, including the mastodon and mammoth. These ancestors of the elephant were fourteen feet tall and had huge tusks. They also were covered in shaggy hair that kept them warm in the cold weather.

How the First People Migrated to North America

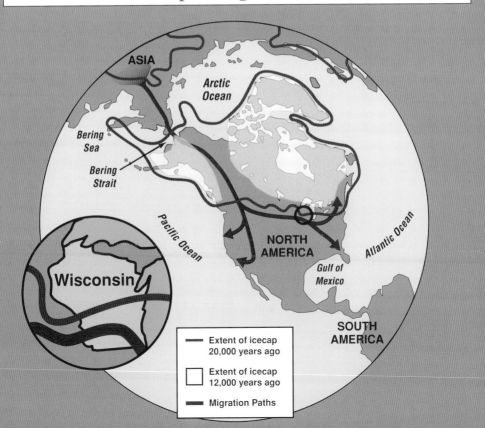

The now extinct mammoth roamed the plains of northern Wisconsin during the Ice Age. The wildlife population changed as Wisconsin's climate warmed.

The Ice Age Ends

Life began to change in Wisconsin about six thousand years ago after the glaciers had melted. As it became warmer, larger animals such as the mammoth disappeared, and smaller ones such as deer, black bear, and beaver began to appear. The American Indians hunted these animals, killing them with wooden clubs and spears. The native tribes also caught fish.

Wisconsin Indians learned new and better ways to do tasks. This made their lives easier. They built more comfortable homes. These were made of poles with animal skin or tree bark stretched over them as a roof. The tribes began to eat more food that grew in the wild, such as rice, and discovered how to make flour by grinding nuts and seeds with a stone. It is believed they made boats by stretching animal skin or tree bark over wooden frames. The boats helped them travel more easily on Wisconsin's many lakes and rivers.

Some hunters who lived in northern Wisconsin during this period are called the Old Copper Indians. They made weapons and tools from chunks of copper metal they found near Lake Superior. The copper was soft enough so that they could beat it into the shape of axes and knives. The Old Copper Indians were the first Native Americans in Wisconsin to make items out of metal.

Woodland Indians

The Woodland period in Wisconsin began about two thousand years ago. Although Native Americans still hunted for much of their food, they also grew some crops, such as corn. They made pottery, lived in larger groups in small settlements, and developed religious beliefs. Woodland Indians resided mostly in valleys along rivers or on the shore of Lake Michigan.

Woodland Indians built burial mounds to protect the spirits of tribal members when they died. They also created **effigy mounds** in the shapes of birds, animals, and people. Effigy mounds were placed on high ground near rivers and lakes in

Wisconsin's Woodland Indians made effigy mounds, like the one seen here in the shape of a bird.

southern Wisconsin. It is believed the mound shapes represented spirits sacred to the Indians. One mound that looks like a huge bird still exists today near Madison, the state capital. The figure is six feet high and has a wingspan of more than six hundred feet.

Newcomers to Wisconsin

About one thousand years ago a different group of Indians migrated to Wisconsin. They traveled up the Mississippi River and other waterways in search of food and new places to live. These newcomers also hunted and fished, but most of the food they ate grew naturally. They also planted and harvested corn, beans, and squash.

Groups of one hundred or more people lived in large villages. Some of the villages were protected by tall wooden fences. The houses they lived in were called **wigwams**. They were made of poles bent into a frame with a round top. The top was covered with birch bark and the sides were mats made of cattails or other reeds. The Indians also made mats to cover the wigwam's floor.

These Indians had a new, more efficient hunting weapon. They had learned to make bows that shot arrows with stone points. The most important animal they hunted was deer. The native people used deerskin to make clothes and blankets to stay warm. Deerskin was also used to make **moccasins** to protect their feet. During the cold winter

Early Wisconsin Indians stretched and dried animal skins during the tanning process.

months, the Indians placed rabbit fur inside their moccasins to make them warmer.

The process of preparing deer hides for use was called **tanning**. It was a hard job. The first step was to scrape the hair from the outside of the hide. This was done with stone tools. The Indians then soaked the hide in a mixture of water and other ingredients. The hide was then stretched, pounded, and finally dried over smoky fires to soften it. Tanning made the deerskin very easy to shape into clothing, pouches, or other useful items.

Many Tribes

By 1600 an estimated 1 million to 2 million Native Americans lived in the vast land that one day became the United States. About twenty thousand of those lived in Wisconsin. By that time four major Wisconsin tribes existed. The Ojibwa, also known as the Chippewa, lived in various parts of the state. The Potawatomi were concentrated in the southeast. The Menominee lived mainly in the Fox River valley in the northeast. The Ho-Chunk, also known as the Winnebago, lived throughout southwestern Wisconsin.

Chief Souligny (left) and Chief Oshkosh were respected leaders of Wisconsin's Menominee Indian tribe during the 1800s.

Other smaller Wisconsin tribes included the Fox, Kickapoo, Ottawa, and Sauk. Some Sioux lived in northwestern Wisconsin, but in this period they were gradually being driven west by the Chippewa, who wanted the Sioux land for themselves.

The **culture** of each tribe had evolved slowly over thousands of years. But when European explorers began arriving in the early 1600s, the native way of life began to change more than ever before.

Chapter Two

Explorers and Fur Traders

Jean Nicolet is the first European known to have reached Wisconsin. In 1634 this French **explorer** arrived on Lake Michigan. Nicolet was eventually followed by other French merchants who wanted to trade for furs with Wisconsin Indians. Their arrival opened a dramatic new chapter in Wisconsin's history.

Nicolet

In 1607 the French established a settlement at Quebec in modern-day Canada. Quebec was the first French outpost in North America. From Quebec, the French began trading with Indians and traveling westward to learn more about North America, a huge land Europeans knew almost nothing about.

Like other explorers before him, Nicolet was searching for the **Northwest Passage,** a legendary

French explorer Jean Nicolet is greeted by a group of curious Winnebago Indians in 1634.

sailing route to Asia. For centuries, Europeans had been searching for a way to travel west to Asia so that they could trade more quickly with Asian nations. Even Christopher Columbus had been trying to find a route to Asia when he unexpectedly ran into the American continent. None of the explorers, not even Columbus, knew that North America lay between Europe and Asia, thus barring their way west.

In 1634 Nicolet left Quebec and traveled with Indian guides by canoe to Lake Michigan. No European had ever seen the lake, but Nicolet had heard tales of this huge body of water from Native Americans. The explorer was excited because he thought it might be an ocean leading to Asia, and that he would find the fabled Northwest Passage.

When Nicolet landed on Lake Michigan's northwestern shore in the area known today as Green Bay, he was met by Winnebago Indians. Nicolet, dressed in a colorful gown of oriental design—he had, after all, hoped to find a shortcut to Asia—fired two pistols into the air as a friendly sign of greeting. The Winnebago, however, had never heard guns fired. The loud noises frightened them so much that they ran away. Eventually, however, the Indians returned to inspect the mysterious stranger.

The booming gunshots, Nicolet's strange appearance, and gifts he gave the Winnebago made them think he was a special person, maybe even a god. They were especially amazed by his iron knives, which were much sharper than their stone knives.

Fur Traders

When he learned more about Lake Michigan, Nicolet realized he had failed to find the Northwest Passage. But he was the first European to step ashore in the future state of Wisconsin. He also began to make friends with the Indians so they would be friendly to other Frenchmen who followed. The French wanted to trade with Indians for the furs of animals such as fox, wolf, and beaver. These furs sold for large sums of money in Europe.

It was nearly two more decades, however, before more French traders returned to Wisconsin seeking furs. In 1654, Médard Chouart des Groseilliers and Pierre Esprit Radisson established a **trading post** on the shores of Lake Superior's Chequamegon Bay.

French fur traders carry their canoe over a section of rushing water.

And in 1666, Nicolas Perrot built Fort St. Nicolas near Prairie du Chien.

The French got furs by trading items to the Indians that the native people could use. Iron knives, metal kettles, cloth, blankets, and **muskets** were greatly desired. One of the most popular items were shiny beads, which Indians began using to decorate their clothes and moccasins.

Fur trading created a major change in the way Native Americans lived. Iron knives made it easier for them to cut, cloth made better clothes than deer-hide and animal skins, and muskets made it easier to hunt animals. The Indians soon became dependent on fur trading so they could continue to get these goods that they could not make themselves.

Marquette and Jolliet

In addition to fur traders, French Roman Catholic priests who wanted to teach Indians about their religion also began coming to Wisconsin. These men were called **missionaries**. The first in 1661 was Father Rene Menard. Another was Father Jacques Marquette, a Jesuit priest who was also a famous explorer.

In May 1673, Marquette, a skilled mapmaker, and Louis Jolliet set out from St. Ignace—a Catholic mission near present-day Mackinac, Michigan—to explore a large new river they had heard about. Indians from farther west called it the "Mes-si-Sipi," and the French wanted to learn more about it.

Indian guides accompany Father Jacques Marquette and Louis Jolliet on their expedition along the Wisconsin River.

Marquette and Jolliet were accompanied by five other men. For many weeks they paddled two canoes over several smaller rivers. Eventually they reached a large river, which Indians called the "Miskonsing." This river is known today as the Wisconsin River. The exploring party traveled down this waterway until June 17, when they came to the spot where it flowed into the much bigger Mes-si-Sipi River.

The French explorers traveled the long waterway as far south as the mouth of the Arkansas River. They decided that the broad, powerful river they renamed "Mississippi" must flow all the way south to the Atlantic Ocean. This was an important discovery about the strange new land's geography.

In exploring the Mississippi River, Marquette and Jolliet also helped give Wisconsin its name. In his report Jolliet wrote the name of the Wisconsin River as Miskonsing, its Indian name. Other Frenchmen later changed the name to "Ouisconsin," a word that is believed to have been derived from the Chippewa "Wees-kon-san," which means "gathering of the waters." In later years, this name would be changed again to Wisconsin and remain the name of the future state.

Indian Warfare

Most Indians liked trading with the French because of the goods they received in exchange for their furs. But some Native Americans fought French fur traders when the traders tried to expand their Wisconsin fur trading business.

Starting in 1700 the Fox tribe warred against the French for three decades. One reason was that the Fox hated the Sioux, whom the French also traded with. The Fox also did not like the way they were treated by the French. Fur traders sometimes cheated Indians out of their furs, beat them if they complained, and mistreated Indian women.

The Fox hated the French so much that they began to kill traders. The two sides then began to fight in a series of battles that extended over many years. In 1716, French officials, in an attempt to regain control of the fur trade, decided to punish the Fox. A French force of two hundred soldiers and nearly one thousand Indian allies were sent to attack the Fox village at Little Lake Butte des Morts near Green Bay.

Wisconsin's Fox tribe hated the Sioux (pictured here playing a ball game), who often traded with the French.

Although the French won the battle, the remaining Fox continued the fight for many years. The Fox finally quit fighting in 1733, when they surrendered in a ceremony at La Baye, the French name for the area known today as Green Bay.

Chapter Three

Settlers Arrive

The French were the first Europeans to come to Wisconsin and establish trading posts at places such as Green Bay, Portage, and Prairie du Chien. However, the French did not have a major impact on Wisconsin's development as a state because France lost control of Wisconsin to England.

France and England had warred with each other in Europe for many centuries. In the 1700s they began competing for control of North America. The British had established a series of thirteen colonies along the East Coast of what would become the United States. The French claimed much of the land along the Mississippi River. Finally in 1754 the two sides clashed over territory rights. This led to the French and Indian War.

The French had many Indian allies in this war, including some from Wisconsin led by trader Charles

Michel de Langlade. His father, Augustin, was French and his mother, Domitelle, was the sister of an Ottawa Indian chief. In 1755, Langlade led a strong force of Indians, many of them Ojibwa from Wisconsin, to help the French defeat British major general Edward Braddock in the Battle of Monongahela. The battle was fought in present-day Pennsylvania.

Although Langlade played a key role in other victories over the British, the French lost the war. In 1763 the Treaty of Paris granted England all the land in North America east of the Mississippi River. As a result, Wisconsin belonged to England.

Charles Michel de Langlade (on left with fist raised) directs an attack during the Battle of Monongahela.

Wisconsin's Place in the United States Today

Alaska

New Hampshire

Minnesota Wisconsin Michigan Vermont

Washington Maine

New York

North Montana Dakota Great Lakes Indiana

Oregon

Massachuse

Idaho South Rhode
Dakota Island
Wyoming

Connecti
Nebraska Iowa New Jersey

Nevada Illinois Ohio

Utah Pennsylvania

Colorado Delaware

California Kansas Maryland

Missouri Kentucky

Arizona New Oklahoma Virginia
Mexico Tennessee West Virginia

Georgia North Carolina

Texas South Carolina

Hawaii

Alabama Florida

Louisiana

Arkansas Mississippi

Wisconsin Changes Hands Again

Although it was a British possession, life in Wisconsin did not change very much. England did not establish a presence in Wisconsin because it was so far away from the settled British colonies along the Atlantic Ocean.

Because of the British neglect, Wisconsin continued to be the temporary home of French traders and missionaries. In 1764 Langlade built a home in Green Bay and became Wisconsin's first permanent European resident.

Despite their victory over the French, the British owned Wisconsin for only a few years. In 1783 the area became part of the United States of America when colonists won their independence from England in the American Revolution.

During the Revolutionary War, Captain George Rogers Clark had commanded an army of colonists and Indians that captured three British strongholds in Illinois and Indiana. Although some of the Native Americans under his command were from Wisconsin, most state Indians fought for the British because they feared the Americans would eventually move west and take their land. The Indians were right, but it did not happen right away.

U.S. Settlers Arrive

Although part of the United States, Wisconsin was ignored for many years by the new nation that owned it. Hundreds of miles west of the original thirteen colonies, Wisconsin was a wilderness too far away to attract new residents from those settled areas. Gradually, however, the East Coast became overpopulated. More and more Americans and immigrants from other countries traveled farther west to find new homes. Some finally made their way to Wisconsin.

The first large wave of settlers came to the southwest part of Wisconsin in the 1820s to mine lead. They built camps that later developed into communities such as Mineral Point. Mining soon became more important to Wisconsin's economy than fur trading. In 1825 southwestern Wisconsin had only two hundred white residents. So many miners arrived in the area that by 1829, several thousand whites lived there.

The first miners were from southern states such as Kentucky and Tennessee. They came in search of new jobs and homes. They were joined by foreigners, including many from Cornwall, a county in England famous for its mining. Immigrants from Germany and Scandinavia also came to mine lead.

Because miners had no place to live when they arrived, they dug into small hills to create primitive shelters. This earned miners the nickname badgers, after the small Wisconsin animal that burrows into the ground to make its home. Wisconsin today is nicknamed the Badger State.

Other Newcomers

Between the 1820s and 1830s thousands of people from other states and foreign countries began moving to Wisconsin. Most of these settlers helped establish communities along either Lake Michigan in the east or the Mississippi River in the west.

One of the cities along Lake Michigan was Milwaukee, which eventually became the state's largest city. Milwaukee grew quickly because it was easy for newcomers to travel there on boats along the Erie Canal and the Great Lakes. Although most newcomers were from states in the New England area, Milwaukee also attracted many German immigrants.

Other cities on Lake Michigan included Green Bay, Sheboygan, and Racine. In the western part of

Wisconsin, La Crosse and Prairie du Chien became important trade centers. They shipped goods south along the Mississippi River to the Gulf of Mexico.

Besides traders and miners, Wisconsin also attracted farmers to the fertile land. So many came that in the 1830s, farming became the region's most important industry. Wheat was the most popular crop, and in a few years Wisconsin was growing more wheat than any other area in the United States.

Farmers, like those seen here, first came to Wisconsin in search of fertile land for growing crops.

Indian Problems

The thousands of people moving to Wisconsin began to crowd the Native Americans off land they had lived on for centuries. Loggers, farmers, and other settlers cut down trees, disrupted Indian hunting grounds, and forced Indians to keep moving their villages to make room for white settlement.

The Indians were so angry that they began to fight back to protect their homes and land. They attacked mining camps and farms, killing the people who lived on their former homeland. Because of this, the U.S. government in 1825 built Fort Crawford in Prairie du Chien and stationed soldiers there to protect settlers.

The Indians were not strong enough to fight the U.S. Army and the many armed white settlers. As a result, in the 1830s, Wisconsin tribes were forced to sell their land to the U.S. government. They then had to either move west of the Mississippi River, where other Indians already lived, or move to Indian reservations the government created in Wisconsin.

Black Hawk War

The most famous conflict between whites and Native Americans involving Wisconsin was the Black Hawk War. It was named after Chief Black Hawk of the Sauk tribe. The Sauk fought the settlers because the tribe had lost its traditional homeland in northern Illinois and southwestern Wisconsin and was forcibly moved west into modern-day Iowa.

On April 6, 1832, Chief Black Hawk led nearly one thousand men, women, and children back across the Mississippi River near the mouth of the Rock River to take back their old tribal land in Illinois.

Sauk Indians retreat from U.S. soldiers during the bloody Battle of Bad Axe.

Indians and whites fought for several months in a series of battles in northern Illinois and Wisconsin. Two soldiers who fought in the Black Hawk War— Abraham Lincoln and Zachary Taylor—were later elected president of the United States.

The Black Hawk War ended on August 1 at the Battle of Bad Axe. After soldiers had chased Chief Black Hawk's tribe into Wisconsin near Prairie du Chien, he tried to surrender. Instead, the whites attacked the Native Americans he led. Native men, women, and children were shot to death or drowned while trying to escape across the Mississippi River. Nearly three hundred Indians were killed in what is considered a tragic **massacre**.

Chapter Four

Wisconsin Becomes a State

The Black Hawk War in 1832 ended Native American resistance in Wisconsin. This made it safe for white settlers to move there, and the region's population grew quickly.

Wisconsin was originally part of the **Northwest Territory,** an area that was eventually carved into the states of Wisconsin, Indiana, Illinois, Michigan, and Ohio. In 1787, Congress had passed the Northwest Ordinance, a law that laid out guidelines for creating states out of this vast wilderness. The first step toward becoming a state was to be named a **territory.**

A Territory

On April 20, 1836, President Andrew Jackson signed a law that formally recognized Wisconsin as a territory. Although its size was reduced when it became a state, the Wisconsin Territory originally included land that today makes up Iowa, Minnesota, and the eastern half of North Dakota and South Dakota. In a July 1836 census, the population for this vast territory was 22,214. More than half those people lived in the lead-mining area, which eventually became part of the state of Wisconsin.

Madison, pictured here in 2001, was chosen as the state capital of Wisconsin in 1836.

President Jackson appointed Henry Dodge the first governor of the Wisconsin Territory. Dodge took office on July 4, 1836, in a noisy, patriotic Fourth of July celebration in Mineral Point. Dodge had moved to Wisconsin in 1827 to open a lead mine, which made him rich. He also became well known as an army officer who fought Native Americans to protect settlers. An important lead-mining community was named after him—Dodgeville.

As a territory, Wisconsin was responsible for making its own laws. Citizens elected the Territorial Legislature with a senate of thirteen members and a house of representatives numbering twenty-six members. The lawmakers met for the first time on October 25, 1836, in Belmont, the small community that had been chosen as Wisconsin's capital. In that first lawmaking session the legislators voted to move the capital to a new community called Madison.

Madison was chosen because it was more centrally located than Belmont. Madison lies on a narrow strip of land that runs between Lakes Monona and Mendota, two of the five lakes that surround it. Madison remains the capital city today.

The Territorial Legislature met in Madison for the first time on November 26, 1838. In the next few years legislators passed laws that made it easier for people to live in Wisconsin. They made improvements in roads and harbors, authorized and levied the first school taxes, and worked hard to gain new residents.

Wisconsin and Milwaukee Grow

Wisconsin soon began to attract tens of thousands of new residents. All were seeking a better life, and they found it in Wisconsin.

Most newcomers were farmers who came because land was plentiful and cheap. Land cost only $1.25 an acre at the time, and people who did not have enough money could buy a farm on credit. Thus, anyone could become a landowner. And the chance for people to own land was the most important factor that led them to keep moving west to **frontier** areas such as Wisconsin.

The Wisconsin community that grew the fastest, however, was Milwaukee, which got its name from an Indian name for a river that runs through the city. In 1761 a British officer was the first to write down the name of the river, which he said was Milwacky. The spelling of this name was changed over the years to become Milwaukee.

The first Europeans to come to Milwaukee were fur traders in the 1600s. In 1818 Solomon Juneau, a Frenchman, began a permanent trading post in Milwaukee. By 1837 the post had several hundred residents. Within six years Milwaukee's population had grown to more than three thousand, and by 1848 fourteen thousand people were living there. In 1846, Milwaukee had been formally recognized by the Territorial Legislature as a city, and fur trader Solomon Juneau was elected its first mayor.

Early Wisconsin farmers used looms like this one to spin wool for making clothes.

Milwaukee grew quickly because it had a natural bay in which ships could dock. This helped it become a rich and important port city. And it was much cheaper and quicker at the time to transport merchandise on ships instead of hauling it overland. The most important products shipped from Milwaukee were wheat, flour, and lead.

Most of the new Milwaukeeans were from New England states, but in the mid-1840s the city began attracting thousands of immigrants from Germany. In the decades to come, these newest residents made

Milwaukee the most German of all American cities. The Germans brought beer-making skills from their homeland, and the city quickly became one of the nation's largest beer-producing cities.

Becoming a State

By 1846, Wisconsin's population had grown to more than 155,000 residents. In April of that year, Wisconsin voters agreed with state officials that their territory should become a state. This was an important step for Wisconsin. Being a state meant that residents would officially become citizens of the United States.

The port city of Milwaukee, pictured here in 1990, is situated on the shores of Lake Michigan.

This German-style farmhouse is similar to those built by early German immigrants to Milwaukee.

Before that could happen, however, Wisconsin needed a **constitution** that outlined the state's laws. Members of a constitutional convention began meeting in Madison on October 5 to create this important document. It took these officials seventy-two days, many of which were filled with bitter debate, to reach an agreement on a constitution.

This first attempt to draft a constitution was rejected by state voters in April 1847. The constitution was voted down because some of it was controversial. For example, it granted married women the right to own property independently of their husbands. This was a very experimental idea for the time, and the voters—all of whom were male—did not like it.

A second version of the document dropped that proposal and several other controversial measures. It was approved by about two-thirds of the territory's voters in March 1848. This cleared the way for Wisconsin to become a state.

On May 29, 1848, President James K. Polk signed a bill accepting Wisconsin as the nation's thirtieth state. The state legislature met on June 5 of that year, and Nelson Dewey was inaugurated as Wisconsin's first governor. Statehood led to more people moving to Wisconsin, and by 1850 the new state's population had reached 305,000. The Badger State, Wisconsin's nickname, continued to grow and prosper in the future.

Facts About Wisconsin

State motto: Forward

State nickname: Badger State

State song: "On, Wisconsin!"

State capital: Madison

State flower: wood violet

State grain: corn

State bird: robin

State animal: badger

State wildlife animal: white-tailed deer

State domesticated animal: dairy cow

State tree: sugar maple

State fish: muskellunge

State mineral: galena

State rock: red granite

State symbol of peace: mourning dove

State insect: honey bee

State beverage: milk

State dance: polka

Glossary

climate: The common weather patterns of an area.

constitution: The basic written laws that guide how a government operates.

culture: The customs and beliefs that guide the way people live.

effigy mounds: Mounds shaped like an animal or human.

explorer: A person who finds and visits new places for the first time.

extinct: No longer existing.

frontier: Wilderness areas.

glaciers: Huge sheets of ice hundreds of feet thick.

Ice Age: A period of Earth's history during which glaciers covered much of the northern United States.

immigrant: A person who comes to a country to take up permanent residence.

massacre: The unjustified murder of a large number of people.

migrated: Moved from one area to another to find a new place to live.

missionaries: People who try to teach religion to another person.

moccasins: Shoes made of deer hide.

muskellunge: A large, fierce game fish that weighs up to eighty pounds.

muskets: Old-fashioned rifles.

Native Americans: The first people to live in the United States.

Northwest Passage: A fabled sailing route through North America to Asia.

Northwest Territory: The area that yielded the states of Wisconsin, Indiana, Illinois, Michigan, and Ohio.

tanning: The process of preparing an animal hide for use.

territory: A section of the United States that is not yet part of one of its states.

trading post: A building or settlement where white traders bought furs from Native Americans.

wigwams: Homes made of bark, animal skins, and other materials.

For Further Exploration

Lenore Herrige Burckel, *Wisconsin: Yesterday and Today*. Morristown, NJ: Silver Burdett, 1985. A well-documented treatment of the past and present history of Wisconsin.

Bettina Ling, *From Sea to Shining Sea: Wisconsin*. New York: Childrens Press, 2002. A brief history of Wisconsin that also provides information about the state today and the people who live there.

Howard Mead, Jill Dean, and Susan Smith, *Portrait of the Past: A Photographic Journey Through Wisconsin*. Madison, WI: Wisconsin Tales and Trails, 1971. This book uses old photographs to trace the state's history.

Richard Hamilton Smith, *Ah, Wisconsin!* Madison, WI: Wisconsin Tales and Trails, 1990. Many wonderful pictures and a lively text describe life in Wisconsin.

Index

Picture Credits

About the Author

Michael V. Uschan has written more than twenty books on a wide variety of subjects. In 2001 he won the Council for Wisconsin Writers Juvenile Nonfiction Award for his book, *The Korean War*. Mr. Uschan began his career as a writer and editor with United Press International, a news wire service. Journalism is sometimes called "history in a hurry." Mr. Uschan considers writing history books a natural extension of skills he developed in his many years as a working journalist. He and his wife, Barbara, reside in Franklin, Wisconsin.